Cool

OUTDOOR
ACTIVITIES

Great Things to Do in the Great Outdoors

Alex Kuskowski

An Imprint of Abdo Publishing
abdopublishing.com

abdopublishing.com

Published by Abdo Publishing, a division of ABDO,
PO Box 398166, Minneapolis, Minnesota 55439.
Copyright © 2016 by Abdo Consulting Group, Inc.
International copyrights reserved in all countries. No
part of this book may be reproduced in any form without
written permission from the publisher. Checkerboard
Library™ is a trademark and logo of Abdo Publishing.

Printed in the United States of America,
North Mankato, Minnesota
062015
092015

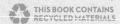
THIS BOOK CONTAINS
RECYCLED MATERIALS

Content Developer: Nancy Tuminelly
Design and Production: Jen Schoeller, Mighty Media, Inc.
Series Editor: Liz Salzmann
Photo Credits: Frankie and Maclean Potts, Jen Schoeller,
Shutterstock

The following manufacturers/names appearing in this
book are trademarks: 3M™ Scotch®, DecoArt® Patio Paint
Outdoor™, Duck Tape®, Elmer's® Glue-All®, Franklin
Sports®, Krylon® ColorMaster™, Rust-oleum® Painter's
Touch®, Scribbles®, Sharpie®, Thompson's® WaterSeal®

Library of Congress Cataloging-in-Publication Data
Kuskowski, Alex.
 Cool outdoor activities : great things to do in the great
outdoors / Alex Kuskowski.
     pages cm. -- (Cool Great Outdoors)
 Includes index.
 Includes webography.
 ISBN 978-1-62403-696-5
 1. Outdoor games--Juvenile literature. I. Title.
 GV1203.K95 2016
 796--dc23
                    2014045311

To Adult Helpers:

This is your chance to inspire kids to get outside! As children complete the activities in this book, they'll develop new skills and confidence. They'll even learn to love and appreciate the great outdoors!

Some of the activities in this book will require your help, but encourage kids to do as much as they can on their own. Be there to offer guidance when needed, but mostly be a cheerleader for their creative spirit and natural inspirations!

Before getting started, it helps to review the activities and set some ground rules. Remind kids that cleaning up is mandatory! Adult supervision is always recommended. So is going outside!

CONTENTS

Get Out!

*E*ver heard this before? "You kids need to go outside and get some fresh air!" Of course you have. You've probably heard it more than you want to. And you've probably been hearing it your whole life. But here's the thing. It's actually true!

We spend most of our lives inside. Take a second to count the hours. You sleep inside. You eat inside. You study inside. That's life in the 21st century.

You've got to get out!

There are a lot of fun outdoor activities you can try. You can make a giant tic-tac-toe board. You can test your aim with a squirt gun. It all happens outside. And it's all good. They don't call it the great outdoors for nothing!

WHAT'S SO GREAT ABOUT

The benefits of being outside are endless. Here's a quick look at what time spent outdoors can do for your body, mind, and spirit!

THE GREAT OUTDOORS?

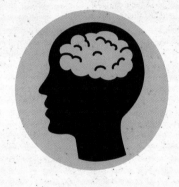

BODY

Playing outside helps you build an active, healthy body. It even strengthens your bones and improves your vision!

MIND

Is your mind racing? Exposure to nature reduces anxiety. And students at schools with outdoor education programs score higher on tests!

SPIRIT

Your stress levels fall within minutes of seeing green spaces. Nature helps us stay in balance!

You Gotta
LIGHTEN UP!

What's another great thing about the great outdoors? Being outside exposes us to the sun's natural light.

The Benefits of
NATURAL LIGHT

Vitamin D

Natural light gives us **vitamin** D. Vitamin D keeps our bodies strong!

Sleep Regulation

Exposure to sunlight helps regulate our sleeping patterns. The more you are outside, the easier it is to fall asleep!

Mood Enhancement

Being outside affects the brain. It activates the parts associated with balance and happiness.

The War on
CABIN FEVER

Cabin fever can happen if you are inside too long. It often happens during the winter. But it can strike during any season. Cabin fever makes you short-tempered. Don't let it happen to you!

Think about the things you do each day. Can you do any of them outside? Ask if you can study or have dinner outside. Tell your family the war on cabin fever is on! Are you reading this book inside? If so, get up and head for the door. Beat cabin fever before it starts!

Did You Know? Doing something inside is not the same as doing it outside. Scientists studied the difference between walking inside and walking outside. They compared people who walked outdoors with people who walked on treadmills. The people who walked outdoors felt better.

ARE YOU READY?

☑ **Check the Weather.** Check the forecast before you begin any outdoor adventure!

☑ **Dress Appropriately.** Dress in layers! Be prepared for a **variety** of temperatures.

☑ Bring Water. It's important to drink enough water, especially if it's hot out.

☑ Get Permission. Some of the activities in this book require adult **supervision**. When in doubt, ask for help!

Now let's get out and enjoy the great outdoors!

Materials

Here are some of the things you'll need.

beans

bowl

bucket

cardboard box top

clear tape

concrete paving block

craft glue

drinking straw

duct tape

felt

foam block

foam brush

golf tees

index cards

newspaper

paintbrush

paper

patio paint

permanent
marker

Ping-Pong balls

puffy paint

ruler

scissors

shovel

rocks

shower curtain
liner

sponges

spray paint

spray sealer

stainless steel
water bottle

string

twine

water gun

wooden coffee
stir sticks

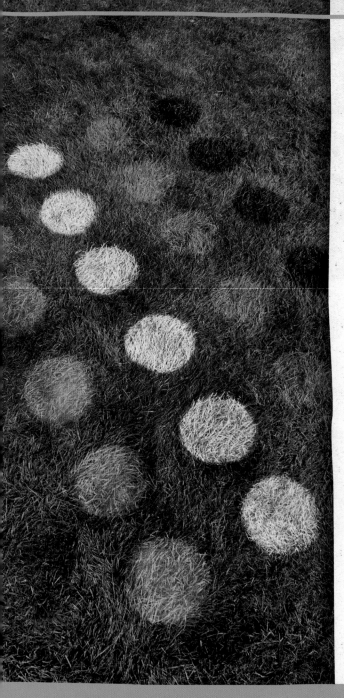

BACKYARD
twist-it

Have fun, but don't get twisted!

Materials

2 bowls
cardboard box top
pencil
scissors
red, yellow, green & blue spray paint
ruler
index cards
markers

1   Set a bowl upside down on the box top. Trace around the bowl. Cut out the circle.

2   Place the box top outside on the grass. Paint the grass inside the circle red.

3   Measure 6 inches (15 cm) from the side of the circle. Paint another circle. Repeat until there are six red circles in a straight line.

(continued on next page)

4 Paint a row of blue circles next to the red circles. Space the blue row 6 inches (15 cm) from the red row.

5 Paint a row of yellow circles next to the blue row.

6 Paint a row of green circles next to the yellow row. Let the paint dry.

7 Write "left hand," "left foot," "right hand," and "right foot" on index cards. Put them in a bowl.

8 Write "red," "yellow," "blue," and "green" on index cards. Put them in the other bowl.

9 One person is the caller. He or she draws a card from each bowl. He or she reads each card aloud.

10 Everyone places the matching body part on the correctly colored circle.

11 The caller picks two more cards. Everyone follows the new directions. They can only move the hand or foot specified on the card.

12 Keep going until someone falls over. It's his or her turn to be the caller.

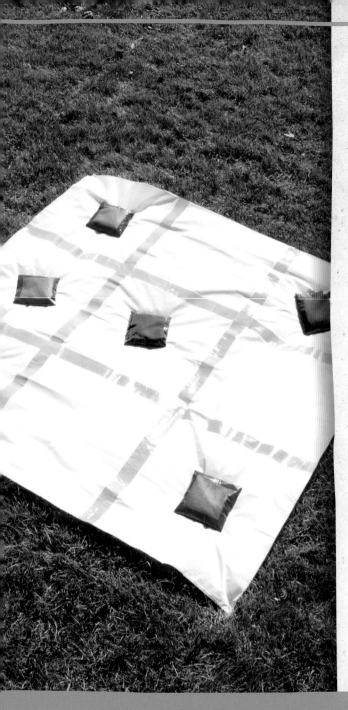

GIANT
tic-tac-toe

Make this game
larger than life!

Materials

blue & red felt
ruler
scissors
blue, red & green duct tape
beans
shower curtain liner
permanent marker

1 Cut two 7-inch (18 cm) squares out of blue felt. Cut four 8-inch (20 cm) pieces of blue duct tape.

2 **Stack** the felt squares. Lay one edge of the squares along a piece of tape. Fold the tape over the edge of the felt. Trim off the extra tape. Cover two more edges with tape the same way.

3 Put beans between the felt squares. Put tape over the open edge of the square.

4 Repeat steps 1 through 3 to make four more blue beanbags. Then make five red beanbags.

5 Cut a 60-inch (150 cm) square out of the shower curtain liner. Lay it flat. Draw a **grid** of nine equal squares on the curtain. Cover the marker lines with duct tape.

6 Stand a few feet away from the curtain. Take turns tossing the bags at the board. Try to make a row of the same color. It can be across, down, or **diagonal**.

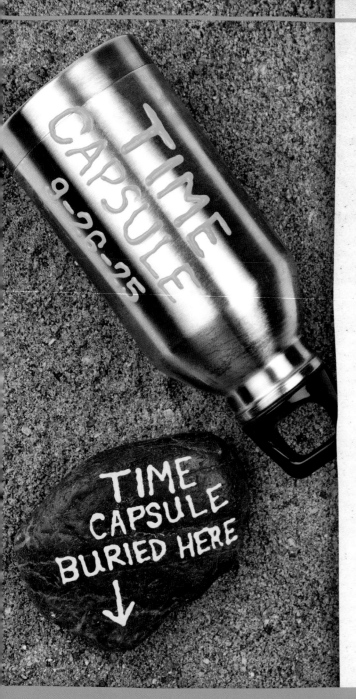

BURY A
time capsule

**Write your message
to the future!**

Materials

newspaper
stainless steel water bottle
puffy paint
large rock
small personal items
shovel

1   Cover your work surface with newspaper. Lay the water bottle on its side. Hold it firmly. Write "time capsule" on the bottle with puffy paint. Add the date you plan to dig up the capsule. Let the paint dry.

2   Paint "time capsule buried here" on the rock. Let the paint dry.

3   Fill the time **capsule** with things you find important. Put in toys or tools. Add a picture of your friends or family. Write a letter to the future. Add current newspaper clippings. Screw the cap of the bottle on tightly.

4   Pick a safe spot to bury the capsule. Get **permission** to bury it there. Dig a hole. Put your time capsule in the hole. Replace the dirt. Put the rock over the hole.

WATER
challenge

Materials

12-inch (30 cm) foam block
duct tape
permanent marker
ruler
5 golf tees
5 Ping-Pong balls
water gun

1 Wrap duct tape around the foam block. Cover all sides completely.

2 Draw five dots across one side of the block. Make the first dot 1 inch (2.5 cm) from one edge. Space the marks 2½ inches (6 cm) apart.

3 Push a tee into the block at each mark. Push the tees in about 1 inch (2.5 cm).

4 Take the block outside. Set it on the ground. Place a Ping-Pong ball on each tee. Shoot the balls off the tees with the water gun.

TIP

Try the Water Challenge in water. The foam block will float!

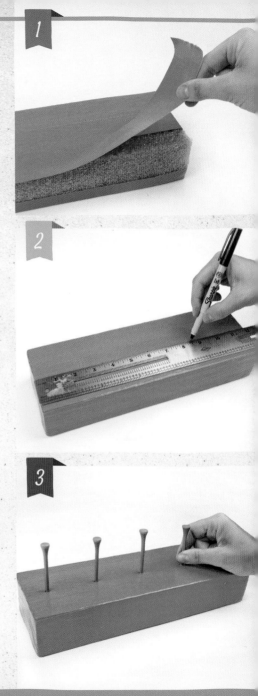

stone
HOPSCOTCH

Make a hopscotch board you can use whenever!

Materials

newspaper
10 concrete paving squares
patio paint
paintbrushes
spray sealer

1   Cover your work surface with newspaper. Paint the paving squares. Use different colors or make them all the same color. Follow the directions on the paint can. Let the paint dry.

2   Paint a number on each square. Number them 1 through 10. Let the paint dry.

3   Spray the sealer on the paving squares. Let them dry completely.

4   Set up the paving squares outside in a **hopscotch** pattern.

SPONGE
blaster

Play sponge dodgeball!

Materials

6 sponges
scissors
twine
bucket
water

1 Cut each sponge **lengthwise** into three equal pieces. Get the sponge pieces wet.

2 Make four **stacks** of two sponge pieces. Set the stacks next to each other.

3 Tie the stacks together in the middle. Wrap the twine tightly around the stacks. Tie a double knot. Trim off the extra twine.

4 Take the sponge ball outside. Fill a bucket with water to dip the sponge ball in.

5 One person tries to hit the others with the wet sponge ball. Whoever gets hit is "it" next.

marvelous
MINI KITE

Send your tiny
kite soaring!

Materials

2 7½-inch (19 cm) wooden coffee stir sticks
paper
ruler
marker
scissors
clear tape
drinking straw
70-inch (178 cm) string

1 Lay a stir stick on a sheet of paper. Make a mark on the stick 2½ inches (6.5 cm) from one end.

2 Cut 1 inch (2.5 cm) off the other stir stick. Lay it across the first stick on the mark. Make sure it is straight and centered.

3 Make marks on the paper at both ends of each stick. Remove the sticks. Use a ruler to draw straight lines connecting the marks. It should make a diamond kite shape. Cut out the kite.

4 Lay the sticks back on the kite. Tape the ends to the corners of the kite. Lay the drinking straw on top of the longer stick. Tape it to the kite.

5 Thread the string through the straw. Tie the ends together to make a big loop.

TIP

Decorate your kite with markers, stickers, ribbons, or glitter.

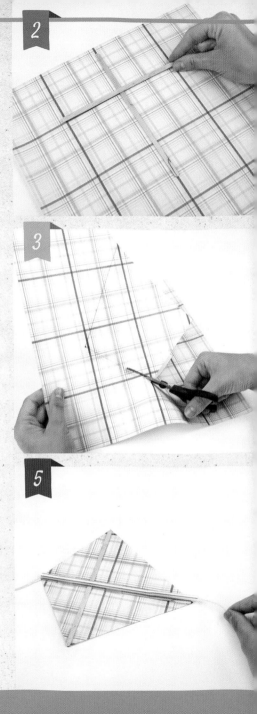

How Great Is the
GREAT OUTDOORS?

*D*id you enjoy the outdoor activities in this book? Did any of them inspire you to do more things in the great outdoors?

There is so much to love about being outside. These activities are just the beginning! Check out the other books in this series. You just might start spending more time outside than inside!

GLOSSARY

appropriately – in a manner that is suitable, fitting, or proper for a specific occasion.

capsule – a type of container.

diagonal – at an angle.

dodgeball – a game in which the players try to hit each other with a ball.

grid – a pattern with rows of squares, such as a checkerboard.

hopscotch – a game played by jumping on numbered squares.

lengthwise – in the direction of the longest side.

permission – when a person in charge says it's okay to do something.

stack – 1. to put things in a pile. 2. a pile of things placed one on top of the other.

supervision – the act of watching over or directing others.

variety – different types of one thing.

vitamin – a substance needed for good health, found naturally in plants and meats.

Websites

To learn more about Cool Great Outdoors, visit **booklinks.abdopublishing.com**. These links are routinely monitored and updated to provide the most current information available.

Index